HOTEL BOY

Books by Curt & Gita Kaufman

Rajesh
Hotel Boy

WITHDRAWN

```
PZ 7 .K38 Ho

Kaufman, Curt.

Hotel boy
```

DATE DUE

WITHDRAWN

GAYLORD · PRINTED IN U.S.A.

HOTEL BOY

by Curt & Gita Kaufman

With photographs by Curt Kaufman

ATHENEUM   New York   **1987**

*To Leland Jacobs, Ph.D., Professor Emeritus of Education, Teachers College, Columbia University
and
Max Stern, M.D., Clinical Associate Professor Emeritus, College of Medicine (New York City), State University of New York*

Two Great Teachers

Text copyright © 1987 by Curt and Gita Kaufman
Photographs copyright © 1987 by Curt Kaufman
All rights reserved.
No part of this book may be reproduced or transmitted in any form or by any means, electronic or mechanical, including photocopying, recording, or by any information storage and retrieval system, without permission in writing from the publisher.

Atheneum
Macmillan Publishing Company
866 Third Avenue, New York, NY 10022

Text set by Fisher Composition, New York City
Printed and bound by Maple-Vail, Binghamton, New York
Designed by Mary Ahern
First Edition

10 9 8 7 6 5 4 3 2 1

Library of Congress Cataloging-in-Publication Data

Kaufman, Curt.   Hotel boy.

   SUMMARY: A boy describes what it is like living in a hotel in New York City with his brother and his mother while she waits to find a job and an apartment.
   1. Poor children—New York (N.Y.)—Case studies—Juvenile literature. 2. Welfare recipients—Housing—New York (N.Y.)—Case studies—Juvenile literature. 3. Hotels, taverns, etc.—New York (N.Y.)—Case studies—Juvenile literature. [1. Hotels, motels, etc.—New York (N.Y.) 2. Housing—New York (N.Y.) 3. New York (N.Y.)] I. Kaufman, Gita. II. Title.
HV4046.N6K38   1987   307.3'36   86-25925
ISBN 0-689-31287-3

MY NAME IS HENRI. I'm five years old, and I don't live in a house, or an apartment like all my friends.

I live in a hotel.

My mother says we used to live in South Carolina. But I don't remember it. We moved to Brooklyn when I was only three. Orlando—that's my brother—he came too. But my father stayed in South Carolina.

When we got to New York, Mom tried to get a job as a cashier, because she's good with numbers.

But it was hard; she had to take care of me.

My brother and I do lots of things together. He's my friend! I'm glad he is, because I don't have a lot of friends in the hotel.

My mother says the other kids fight too much.

We didn't always live in a hotel. We used to live in an apartment like everyone else. But one day, when we came home from Grandmother's, our house was on fire.

All our clothes were burned. All our toys were burned. All our schoolbooks were burned.

Our home was gone!

All we had were the clothes we had on, and each other!

When Mom came home, she cried at first. But then she smiled because she was glad that Orlando and I were OK.

Mommy talked to someone who works for the city called a social worker.

The social worker told Mom there are many people who are burned out of their homes by fire. The city tries to help them find new apartments. Until the apartments are ready many burned out people have to live in special hotels.

First the city moved us into a hotel across the river, in a part of New York City called Manhattan.

Then after a few days, they moved us to another one.

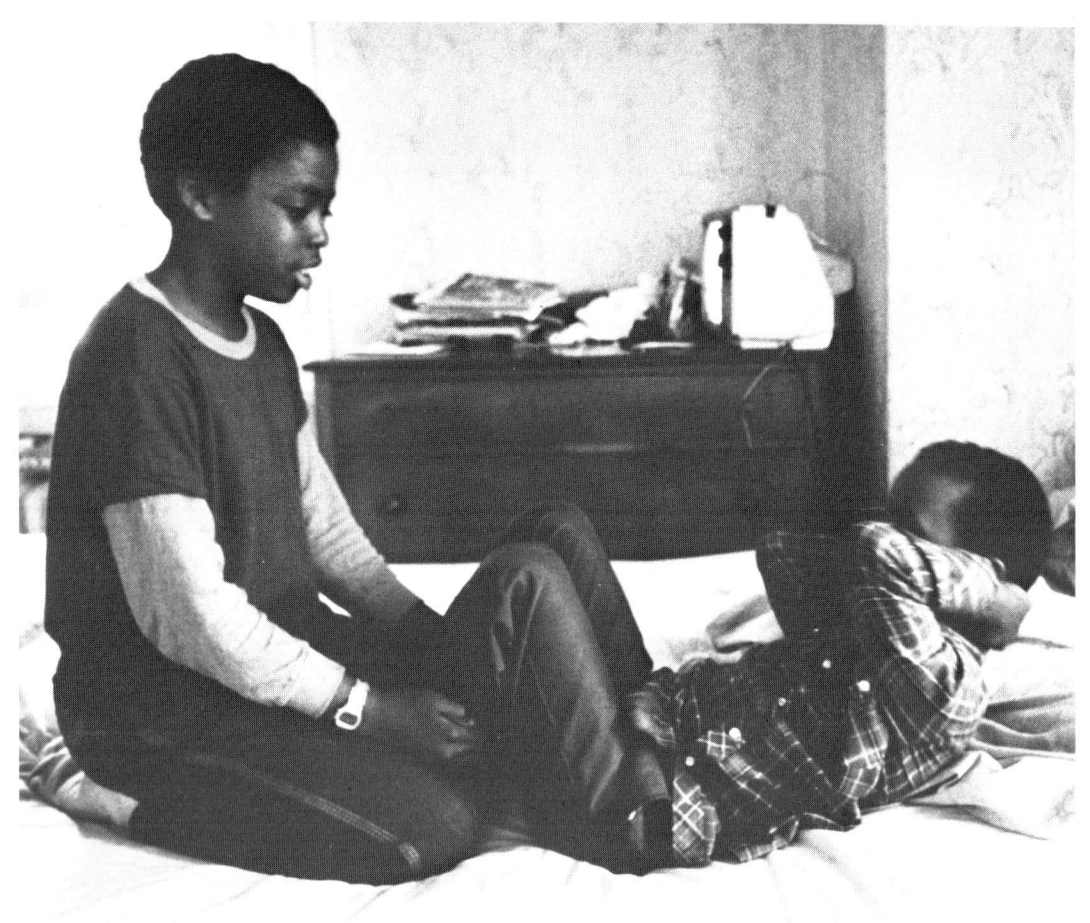

Here's where I live now.

We're very crowded because the kitchen, the bedroom and living room are in one little room. Mommy has to do the laundry in the bathroom.

Mommy says we will be moving to a new apartment just like the one we had before. I hope it's soon because I miss my toys and my books and having my own room.

It's always crowded in our hotel room so Orlando and I either watch TV or play on the bed.

Sometimes I play with my toys. There are pieces from different games—like Leggo, Scrabble and Tinker Toys.

Mom finds them and brings them home to Orlando and me. We keep them in a bag.

One day, I was breakdancing in the hotel lobby. But Mr. Watson, who guards the hotel, told me to play outside with my friends.

It's hard to make new friends.

Today I am at a new school. I hope the kids will like me.

I *did* make friends at school!
Here I am at the art table with Trilby.
I am the clean-up monster.
I wish I could stay in school till ten o'clock at night!

Mommy met me after school, and we walked home together. I told her about my day.

She smiled, but she's sad too. She's still having trouble finding a job.

Broadway is our playground.

Orlando and I see many interesting things here!

. . . a big motorcycle!

. . . all the animals in the pet store!

mmm . . . I wish I could have one of those cakes!

I like being on the street instead of in our room. It's too crowded when all three of us are there together.

When we get outside, Orlando and I like to run, and run, and run.

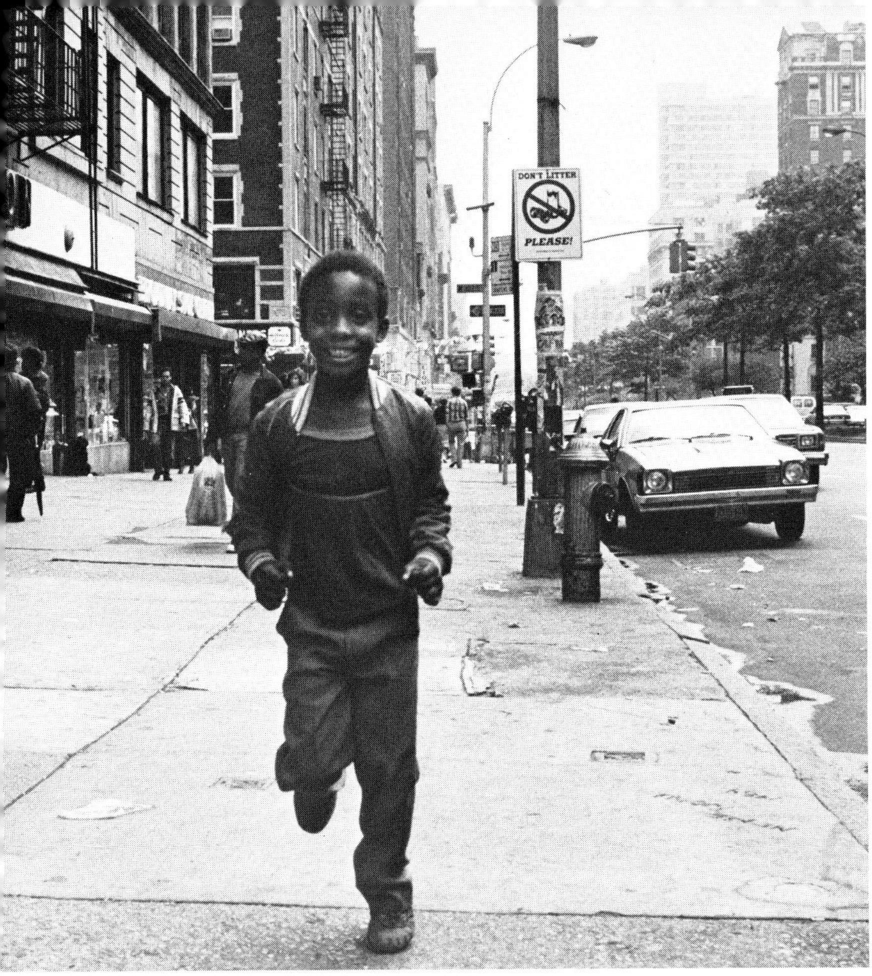

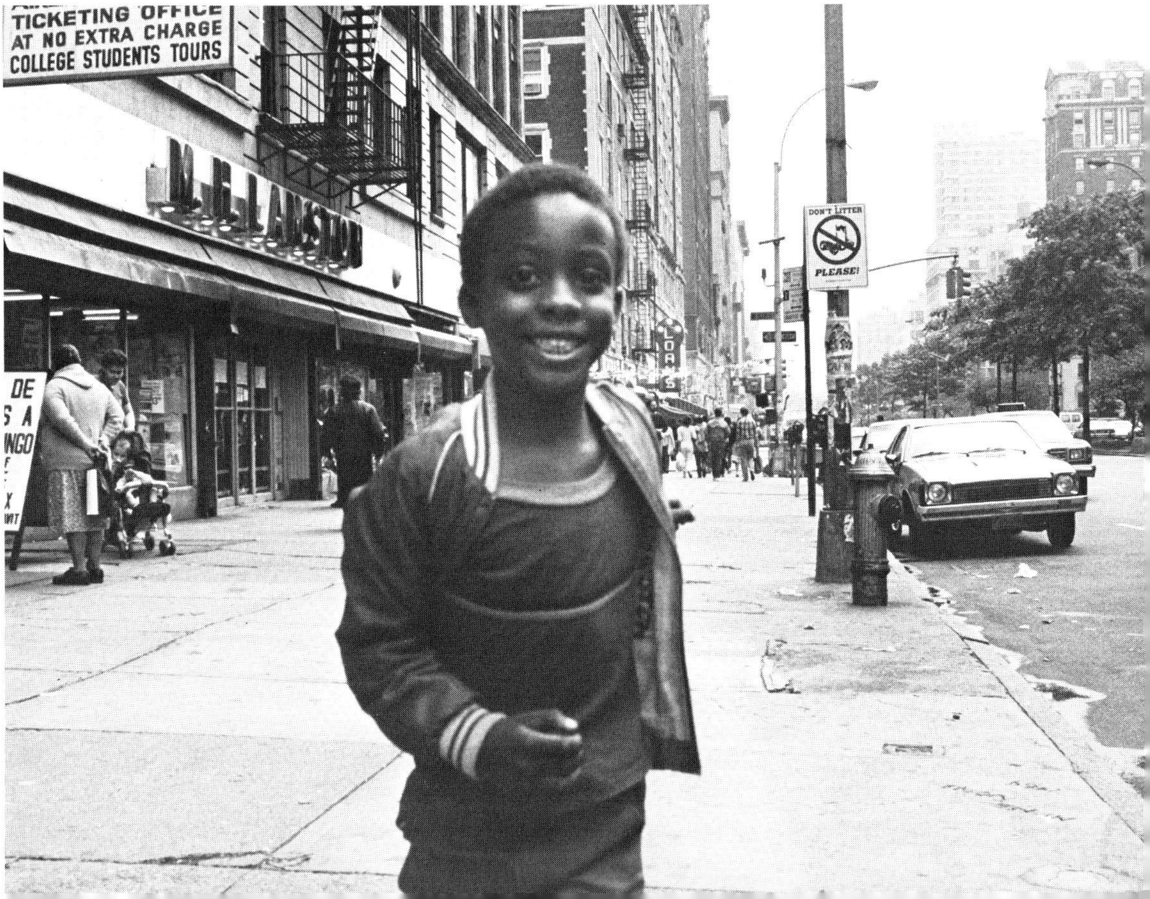

Sometimes we get hot running and Mommy gives us money for ice.

One day, Mom took us for pizza and a soda. While I was eating my pizza, Mom asked the man at the counter for a job as a cashier.

The man said he didn't need anyone.

One weekend Mom, Orlando and I took a long subway trip to the zoo.

We rode a camel!

I looked at the animals through the bars, and wondered how I looked to them.

Orlando and I ran up over a rock. We were having so much fun we kept on running and running. When we stopped by the wolves' cage, Mommy was lost.

But Orlando said not to be afraid because he'd take care of me until we found Mom again.

I was scared though, until we found her. I told her not to get lost again.

She hugged me and changed my shirt in the bathroom because I was all sweaty.

It was a big day for me. I was tired on the ride home.

I told about the zoo in school, and I knew

the answers to all the questions the teacher asked.

Then, the teacher told us that Saskia, my partner, is leaving and we are having a party for her in the park.

Saskia is Irish and she's going back to Ireland.

After the party, I gave some of my potato chips to the other kids while I was waiting for Mommy.

It was sad to say good-bye to Saskia.

Later when Mom and I went out shopping, I told her about Saskia and the party.

She knew how I felt because she's still having trouble getting a job.

Today is my birthday. I'm six years old.
Mom bought a beautiful birthday cake.
She lit the candles for me. I'm going to blow them all out and make a wish.
I'm going to wish for a new place to live.

The room was crowded and Orlando and I were getting restless. We tripped over each other a lot so Mom took us to the park to play.

We ran and jumped.

We threw stones. . .
. . . and rested against a tree.

That night Mom read me a story before I went to bed. Orlando listened too.

She tries to read to me every night.

And then I went to bed.
   There is nothing much else to do when we're all in the room.

I really feel happy today. The social worker told Mom they're getting an apartment ready for us in Brooklyn. Orlando and I will have our own room!

And I learned how to tie my own shoe.

The big day is here!
Mom packed all our things in boxes.
We made a lot of trips on the subway carrying them.

Here we are at our new home! Plenty of space for Orlando and me!

I'll miss the friends I made. But Mommy said that when she gets that job in Manhattan she'll let me visit them sometimes.

Monday I start my new school, and I'm going to make new friends all over again!